To:

_____

Your Life Has a Purpose!

Finding Your WHY

*"Many plans are in a man's mind,
but it is the Lord's purpose for him
that will stand."*
Proverbs 19:21

Finding Your WHY

Finding
Your
"WHY"

Discover Your Purpose

By Mike Rodriguez

2015

Finding Your WHY

Tribute Publishing

Finding Your WHY
First Edition February 2015

All Worldwide Rights Reserved
ISBN: 978-0-9906001-2-1
ISBN: 978-0-9906001-3-8

Printed in the United States of America.

In God We Trust.

To Bonnie,
My gorgeous wife, the love of my life and
the mother of our 5 daughters.
You are the key God gave to me to find my WHY.
I love you so much.

To Our Daughters,
Lauren, Lexi, Linsey, Leia and London.
You should know that each one of you has given me so
much inspiration. I love you.

Finding Your WHY

CONTENTS

PROLOGUE

It was about an hour or so into the New Year on January 1, 1968.

It was a typical winter in Germany, the temperature was very cold, a white blanket of snow was still falling and ice had covered the ground. Antonio was stationed in Baumholder due to Army obligations with his lovely wife Helen. They had a familiar resemblance to Lucy and Ricky Ricardo from the television show "I love Lucy." They enjoyed being with each other. On this particular night they were out celebrating the New Year together. To be honest, Tony was the only one really celebrating. Helen was primarily focused on finalizing her nine months of pregnancy. She patiently watched her husband chase balloons around the dance floor, while listening to Bobby Bare sing "500 Miles." Tony's goal was to capture a balloon as a prize for Helen, all while he balanced a silver stainless steel ice bucket on his head.
And then it happened.

Helen urgently called out to Tony to let him know that she was going into labor. Tony responded quickly and escorted her to their car, desperately off to find a hospital for his beloved pregnant wife. As they drove down the snow covered road, Helen called for Tony to slow down.

Right about that same time they started slipping off the icy road, eventually sliding into a tree. Miraculously they were both unhurt, but by now Helen's water had broken.

Tony was full of adrenaline and managed to maneuver the vehicle back onto the road. In his desperation, he drove the car right through a checkpoint at the local military base security gate, prompting officers to follow him to the only local medical facilities, which happened to be a small dispensary. This dispensary was a tiny medical facility which provided the most basic primary healthcare services to the rural community.

Upon arriving, they were informed that the only medical personnel available to deliver a baby was a Dentist. The staff was obviously not expecting critical patients considering the weather and the New Year's celebration, but it was too late to turn back now.

Helen's fifth child was memorably born, delivered by a dentist. This New Year's Baby, the first baby of the year, was named Michael Alan Rodriguez. That is me.

Ironically, this true and tumultuous journey to my birth would practically set the stage for the young adult years of my life. I would make poor decisions, leading to key distractions that would always sidetrack my path and keep me from stepping into my true purpose.

I would experience many failures, most of them as a result of those poor decisions, but also because of my inability to look at the big picture and to know or even understand my true potential. I was too busy living my life on my terms to even stop and listen for the amazing plans that God had in store for me. He was talking to me, I just wasn't listening.

God had a plan and a purpose for me and He has one for you too.

I am writing this book with the faith that I will be able to connect with people. Those who are in the same places that I have been at various times of my life or those who feel that they can just do something more with their life.

My goal is to share a plan of action that will provide a road map for you to follow, to uplift you out of your current situation and into your purpose.

I have overcome failure after failure in my life, only to realize success again and again. Without any business experience, I was still able to get a sales job in corporate America and work my way up. I have been a top performer at many organizations, earning a spot as Number 1 sales person in the United States out of several hundred sales people. I was named manager of the year after consistently being the Number 1 ranked manager in an entire company of 44 sales managers.

I eventually worked my way up to become a Vice President with a corporate telecom organization and I even started and successfully ran my own business in a partnership with Southwestern Bell (now AT&T). I made quite a bit of money and worked extremely hard to make things happen. But I was never truly happy.

Why? Because I wasn't living my purpose.

Instead of focusing on God's plan for my life, I was always an ego based businessman focused on money, using God as only a resource. I had it backwards.

Now, after learning to listen to Him, I have eliminated the things in my life that have kept me from becoming who I was born to be. My life has a whole new meaning and direction. Through following God's will for my life, I am humbled to be a published Author, an internationally known speaker and a professional sales trainer. I have attained the ultimate goals for my life and you can too.

My life's journey, as tumultuous as it has been from birth until being a husband and a father, has been by His design. My life has not defined me, it has refined me for His plans: I have been tasked with helping others to discover their purpose. To find their WHY.

YOU have a purpose... you have a WHY.

*"Your **WHY***

is understanding

God's purpose for your life

and following that purpose

to fill a need in this world."

— Mike Rodriguez

Finding Your WHY

Chapter 1

Your Life

"For I know the plans I have for you,"
declares the Lord,
"plans to prosper you and not to harm you,
plans to give you hope and a future."
-   Jeremiah 29:11

CHAPTER 1 – Your LIFE

Your life is a gift to you.

Where you are in your life right now is only temporary.
It's up to you to let it become permanent.

This applies to all situations and to all people. Whether you are on top of the world right now, facing a tragic loss or even if you feel that you are just existing, it is only temporary. If you are at a point in your life that is not "where" you expected or "what" you expected, that is certainly understandable. It is, however, up to you to let where you are become permanent.

Life doesn't always present good situations, nor are they easy. Regardless of how you view where you are, you must believe that it is happening for a reason. When facing a tough time or going through a bad situation, let yourself feel whatever emotions you are going through, but don't let them overtake you. Tough times will not last.

The majority of the challenges that I have lived through, when I trace them back, were usually a result of the consequences of my decisions (or indecisions). Yet, I have also learned that God places us in situations or allows situations to happen, for us to get through, so He can get through to us. Situations that you are in may not make sense to you today, but they will later on.

CHAPTER 1 – Your LIFE

All of life's experiences serve a higher purpose - to bring us closer to God. He is indeed mysterious and when we seek to understand Him from a human perspective, nothing that has happened or that will happen in our lives could ever make sense, because God is not human. He is the almighty creator of the universe!

I find that most of us rationalize with and analyze our creator, based on what we feel, want, need or hope to happen. This is where we get side-tracked on our journey through life, especially when we are going through tough times.

We must learn to understand that in life, we are either moving closer towards God or we are moving further from Him. Let me clarify that He is always with us and never leaves us. Regardless of where we are in life, what we are doing or what we are going through, he is always there. When we do things to move further away from God, this means that we are choosing to think, speak or act in a way that is not compatible with allowing Him to go to work in our lives. This usually involves us doing something that we shouldn't be doing, having a lack of faith in general or just living our lives our own way, according to the world and our will. Awareness of this, creates an awareness of change.

I will be the first one to agree that initially it will seem very difficult to start making changes in your life.

However, once you make the decision, you will find that living with faith and a positive attitude to change, requires as much energy and effort as living with doubt, worry, fear and uncertainty. Then you realize that you can change.

For a large part of my life, although I was a Christian, I had let the ways of the world influence my thoughts, actions and words. We do live in this world, but we should not become like this world. We need to work every day to include Him, not as an add-on, but as "The One." This doesn't mean that you won't have doubts, worries and fears, but it does mean that you can have peace and faith through your tough times. Your life does have a plan and there is a light at the end of the tunnel.

I know that God has always been with me, all the time. There has never been a doubt in my mind. However, I kept Him at a distance to make sure that I didn't feel too bad about my behavior. At times, when I was strong in my faith, I would let my light shine and I felt wonderful. However, when I wasn't strong, when I wasn't living right or when I was just not being happy, I would make sure that I was keeping Him at a reasonable distance. I did this so I could still feel good about myself. As if He didn't know.

The explanation that I can give is that it was like I was walking through a very long tunnel made of glass, like at an aquarium. The tunnel represented my life's journey.

I would walk down the middle of the tunnel and God was ALWAYS walking at the same pace as me, right next to me, but always on the outside of the glass. Not because He wanted to be there, but because I wouldn't let Him in. The glass allowed me to see Him and be assured of His presence, but it also served the purpose of keeping Him from being too close in my life. I wanted His presence, but not His conviction over me, primarily because I was ashamed of my actions. To others, I am also ashamed to say, that I didn't want to come across as "religious."

Ironically, when I had low points in my life, I would become angry with God for not being with me. How silly was that thinking, because He was always there. It was only when I learned to become obedient and change my life, that I finally learned and made the decision to break down that glass wall. We would no longer be separated. I would welcome Him, because I was no longer ashamed, and I was empowered by this new amazing and peaceful presence.

His love is unconditional. There is nothing that you have done or that you can do to mess it up. Accept this as a truth and remind yourself of this when you are feeling low. When you are down, it's easy to feel hopeless and abandoned. Just know that you are never alone and hope is always present. You only have to believe and seek.

In my new walk, He is still with me and I can still see Him; but now I can feel, know and have a completely different kind of love with him. There are no barriers between us. The reality is that His love has never changed. Mine has.

Most of us live our lives this same way, by using God as a convenience. Sometimes we only call on Him when we are at our darkest moments. It is a truth that no one wants to admit. This is usually apparent when we face some kind of bad or life changing event, usually with undesirable consequences. He is always there for us, but sometimes we are only there, obediently, when we feel the need or when it is convenient for us. This mindset is counter-productive to building the kind of relationship that we need. Turning away from the ways of the world is very hard indeed.

God made you and me and He knows everything about us and everything that will happen in our lives. We have been prepared for every situation that we will encounter, even when we feel like we can't make it. He will never give you more that you can handle. He loves us unconditionally and wants us all of the time, good and bad. He wants you to call on Him when you are at your lowest, but He also asks that you praise Him at your highest! Give thanks and praise during your good times, but also find the strength to give praise and thanks during difficulties, even when you don't understand what is happening or why it is happening. Of course this is easier said than done, but it is in fact a choice.

During good times it's easy to give thanks, yet during difficult times it is equally important to give thanks to God. You are going through whatever it is that you are going through for a reason. He is with you and you must believe that the situation ultimately serves a purpose for your life.

Life's Standards

There is one constant in life: change will happen. Your life involves people, routines, circumstances, events and God's will. With almost all of these, you have limited power in controlling what happens. What you can control is your faith and your attitude about how you respond to what happens to you and your decision to act. Circumstances will happen and things will not always be in your favor. No one plans on leaving the house and getting in a wreck, but it happens. You might go into work and find out randomly that you are laid off, or you might get the surprise gift of a promotion. Things will happen to you, but they are not the standards in your life. They are merely events or circumstances.

To better explain how you should view this as you progress in life, I have created a graph. As you look at the graph, you will notice that there are three lines.

These lines represent measurements of where you are when events happen in your life, with examples.

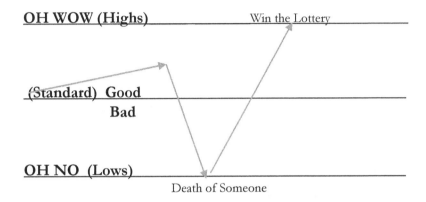

OH WOW (Highs)   Win the Lottery

(Standard) Good
            Bad

OH NO (Lows)

Death of Someone

The Top Line is the "OH WOW" line. Anything from the "Good" line which is above the "The Standard" line, up to this line, would measure positive events that happen in your life.

The Middle Line is the "Standard" line. This represents life as a regular day without any major events.

The Bottom Line, the "OH NO" line, represents the challenges that you face in your life. Anything from the "Bad" line down to this line measures everything negative that happens in your life.

9

If you have a tragic event, say a death in your family, you can see that this can drop you well below your life standard to the "OH NO" line. Likewise, if you have a major victory, like winning the lottery, you can be propelled up to the "OH WOW" line.

In life, you are either moving forward and up or forward and down. We don't move backwards. We simply choose to stay at certain levels depending on the circumstances that we encounter. Right now you are probably saying, I'm not choosing to stay unhappy or mad, things have happened to me! Yes, things may have happened, but you must learn to adjust and choose to move on. This is more relevant when we face a difficult challenge. We might become depressed, create a negative attitude and feel that our life is worthless. We might even feel that we are not even capable of moving forward. This is the point where we stop living and stay low on the chart. The thought of your life being worthless is simply not true, but this is how we get in trouble.

You must take action to remember that God is always with you and He wants you to be happy and productive! You must also believe this and say this to yourself:
All things are temporary! Better, greater and happier times are ahead!

During good times, we have a tendency to recognize, rejoice and praise God when we are above the "standard" line.

CHAPTER 1 – Your LIFE

The challenge with this is we might get an unrealistic expectation of our life and make things appear tougher when you fall again. Enjoy where you are, but understand the nature of the event that you are rejoicing in. Remember, ALL things are temporary in life.

When we fall below the standard line, this is when we start to doubt and question God. We might even become angry. When we get to this point, sometimes we have a tendency to stay there and hold ourselves below life's standards. We might even feel like we have the right to stay down there. You don't.

We must learn to think and believe that everything happens for a reason. A great event is simply that; a great event. It isn't permanent or the new standard in your life. Likewise, a bad event is simply that; a bad event. Neither of them are the standards in your life. You will only stay at a place that you choose to stay at, and you will only stay there as long as you choose to stay there.

Life's events do not happen to define us, they happen to "refine" us. We must keep moving forward and we must keep moving upwards.

"God allows us to go through challenges. Not to DEFINE us, but to REFINE us."

Success

We often equate success with being happy. Please know that this is not necessarily true.

Your happiness is 100% dependent on you, not your circumstances or things. When you consider that "things" do not carry emotion; you can determine that your emotions about "things" are really a direct result of your own conscious or subconscious decisions. If you are an unhappy person, regardless of how successful you become, or how many things you buy, you are still you, so you will probably remain unhappy.

The questions to ask yourself are:

1. How do you define success?
2. How do you define happiness?
3. How will you attain either one?

Success can and usually has different meanings to different people. It is important to find out what motivates you, what your goals are and what you were called to accomplish. You are your own unique person. God made you and He made you for and with a purpose. Sometimes situations that you are in can motivate you and can prompt you to become better.

CHAPTER 1 – Your LIFE

When I was growing up, my father was in the Military. We frequently moved, usually about every two years, living in various places around the U.S. We even lived in Germany. The biggest challenge that I faced growing up was making new friends, since we moved so much.

I learned that if I did not adapt to my environment and take action to initiate conversation to get to know people, that I would be friendless and alone. People have always considered me to be a very outgoing person, an extrovert of sorts, however the reality is that as a child, I subconsciously learned to change my behavior to allow myself to adapt to my situation. I did this so I could be successful in my friendships.

I learned that the pain of being lonely was greater than the pain of forcing myself to be outspoken to total strangers in order to make friends. As a result, I took action to adapt and I was able to make many friends. This behavioral model was an example that I would learn from. It would help to shape my social core and my ability to adapt and overcome my challenges. I taught myself how to become successful in making new friends and I value that.

My point is that success can and will have different meanings to different people. Some people measure success by money, others by fame and some by material possessions.

However, those may not be the true measurements of success for you. If your goal is to be a better husband or wife and you have taken steps to make this happen and your family recognizes it, then you are indeed a success. If you choose to improve your life and you do, then you are successful.

Happiness

Happiness on the other hand is a state of mind, based on your reaction or response to something. Sometimes it might be a very difficult choice for you to be happy, especially if you are going through a hardship. Being sad and staying sad is a difficult mindset to come out of, so you must look inside of yourself, (not outside to things) to find and remember your own happiness. You can have many material things and personal relationships, but if you are not content with your own life, you will still not be happy.

Happiness is not offered by others, nor is it found in things. Buying a material possession or celebrating an event can certainly create joy, but true internal happiness is based on your decision. You must choose to be happy, regardless of your circumstances. Appreciating where you are in life and what you have materialistically, is a big start. Understand that purchasing more items does not bring true happiness.

You may not live or work where you want to and that's fine, but in order to move to the next level, you must learn to appreciate what you have today. God will provide blessings in your life in many ways, but how can He continue to bless you with more opportunity if you cannot appreciate where you already are and what you already have?

When you understand that every situation in your life is merely a stepping stone and part of a plan for greater things, then you start to understand the value and importance of everything in your life.

Everything that you do and every situation that you encounter, is a step that must be taken in order to get to the top of the next step. When you lose the importance of a life's step due to a setback, it will keep you from moving forward and moving closer towards God's plan for your life.

POSITIVE AFFIRMATIONS:

- ➤ I recognize that God is in control of my life.
- ➤ Where I am in my life right now is only temporary.
- ➤ My challenges refine me, they don't define me.
- ➤ I choose to be happy.
- ➤ Things don't bring me happiness, I choose to be happy about things.
- ➤ There is a plan and a purpose for my life.

Chapter 2

Your Navigator

*"In their hearts humans plan their course,
but the Lord establishes their steps."*
- Proverbs 16:9

CHAPTER 2 – Your NAVIGATOR

On the day we are born, how wonderful would it be if we were given a map to visualize the purpose for our life? What if we could see the dangers and challenges that we would encounter? What if we could clearly see our path?

I know that most of us would reroute our maps to avoid obstacles. We would probably select paths that would take us straight to the places that would make us happy. Some of us might even choose a completely different route, taking us somewhere that we think or feel would be better for us. Well here is the reality: that is a "human" life strategy.

As I mentioned earlier, our life is not our life. It was given to us, complete with a roadmap, but of course we do not have the privilege of seeing the roadmap. We must trust in our navigator; the one who holds our roadmap.

Years ago I had to meet a client in a part of the Dallas / Fort Worth area that I wasn't familiar with, so I needed assistance to find my way. I typed the address in my navigation system and proceeded to follow the route that was called out to me by my device. The journey took me down many familiar roads and places that I had seen before. However, before too long I was driving down a deserted road in an area that I wasn't familiar or comfortable with. I knew something was wrong, but I figured that the navigation knew something that I didn't. I trusted it.

CHAPTER 2 – Your NAVIGATOR

About halfway down the dirt road, without any civilization in site, my GPS told me that I had arrived at my destination. I looked around and I was in front of an abandoned gas station. I was frustrated and angry…. and I was lost.

The point is that we have strong faith in electronic navigation systems that were "built by man," to blindly guide us to destinations. Yet, when it comes to faith in our almighty navigator, who built man, we might not have the confidence to even get started! This is completely backwards.

We must trust in our creator to guide our path through the divine plan that He has for our life. We must do this with the same confidence and blind faith that we have in our "man-made" electronic devices. This means that you will encounter obstacles and detours, you will have rest stops and delays, and you will encounter extended visits to fun points of interest. You will also end up at places you don't want to be. Through it all you must believe, you must be strong and you must continue to move forward.

If you are saying to yourself, "But wait a minute, I am WAY off course in my life. How can I ever get back on track?" I would say to you don't worry, don't be concerned and don't be afraid. God's plans are perfect.

Just as a good navigation system will correct your path and make adjustments when you get off course; our father will do the same, as long as you are willing to adjust too.

Life's situations may seem too big for us, but they aren't for Him.

You will find as you read this book that this is a big concept of my own life. I followed many wrong paths and made many decisions that took me way off course; and that is exactly my point. When you follow the truth, He will straighten your path. God lets these things happen as a method to guide us and teach us. They are all part of His plan.

Listen for direction

While I was in college, I was working two jobs. I worked at the local mall at a GNC, pushing vitamin supplements, and then right afterwards, I would run down to the Sears store in the same mall and sell large appliances.

Long days, mundane routine and a true "lack of vision" at college prompted me to be uncertain about my college path. It made me doubt my future. My oldest brother was a store manager of a jewelry store in that same mall and at that time, he appeared to be making good money.

CHAPTER 2 – Your NAVIGATOR

One day as I stopped by to say hi to my brother, I was approached by his boss. He apparently sensed my passion and personality and asked if I would be willing to take a job and move to Tulsa. Being ambitious and considering my current situation at school, the proposition was very appealing. I asked him about the income potential and he told me it would be about 3 times what I was making (which wasn't much). My short sightedness led me to falsely believe that this opportunity was an escape from my misery and a path to the big time! My own misguided, youthful will took over, and I soon left college and took the job.

After several months, the pain of being alone in Tulsa and the sense of not improving, magnified the reality of my bad decision. To top it all off, the money wasn't that great either. However, I decided to stay in the jewelry industry, since it was the only formal training that I had at that time. This was a prime example of making a big move in my life for my benefit and for the wrong reasons. I was fighting to create my own path in life.

After a few more moves, from Tulsa to Austin, I ended up in Dallas. I worked very hard and as a result, shortly thereafter I was promoted to the manager of my own jewelry store. At 20, I was one of the youngest managers in the company, but I wasn't happy. Something was still missing.

I knew that I could do more with my life, I just didn't have a plan, experience or direction. In addition, and unfortunately; I still wasn't listening to God. Thankfully, I was aware of the drive, desires and passion He had placed in me.

I was still going through a very tough time in my life while I was in Dallas. I was lost, lonely and I felt isolated. Strangely enough, deep down inside I knew that something was in store for me and that I had an opportunity waiting, someway or somehow. Even still, I started living my life recklessly and things soon got out of control. One night I carelessly got in an accident that, according to logic, should have killed me.

After the accident, I felt defeated, but I did know that God was still there for me. I got on my knees and I prayed. I asked Him to bring someone into my life to help me get back on track. I was ready to settle down and marry the right girl. I poured my heart out and I cried myself to sleep that night praying. I really wanted to change my life. At the time, I did not know it, but that horrible situation would turn out to be my wonderful turning point. It was a route guidance correction from my navigator to realign my path!

One month later I would meet the most wonderful and beautiful girl that I have ever met in my life. Her name was Bonnie.

Bonnie was beautiful, kind, had values and wasn't like any other girl that I had ever met before. I fell in love instantly and fortunately for me, she fell in love with me too. Now, after meeting her, I was excited and determined to improve. Bonnie completed me and I was renewed, focused now (I thought) and ready to succeed! I sat her down one day and told her that I knew I was meant to do bigger and better things. I told her that I was going to quit my job as a retail manager to pursue those bigger and better things. She said okay and said that she believed in me. At that point, if I had any doubt about marrying her, it was all gone. I knew we were meant for each other, and shortly after, we were married.

My wife Bonnie and I have now been happily married since 1991 and we have five beautiful daughters together.

As I look back on that sorrowful night before I met Bonnie, when I thought that I was alone, I can now say with complete truthfulness and conviction, that God was with me. He did indeed listen to me and He fulfilled my prayer. I just had not been listening to Him. I also now understand that the accident, which led to my call out to Him, was all part of his plan for me to pursue my WHY. Bonnie, through God's foundational plan, has been my motivation and a big part of my purpose to be, do and have more in my life. She was the delivery of a bigger message to me.

The accident and meeting Bonnie, validated to me that I was capable and ready to do bigger and better things with my precious life. The previous problem was that it wasn't painful enough in my life for me to make a change. Once my life got to the point that it was too painful to live the way I was living, I was ready to do anything to change. And I did.

Bonnie and I were ready for big things, all packed up but nowhere to go. I came across an ad for a telecom company that was hiring, but there was a catch. A college degree was required. Uh oh. What would I do? I called a friend who advised me not to embarrass myself. Doubt and uncertainty were rampant in my mind, but as I prayed and listened for direction, I had something inside of me that kept telling me to go to the interview. That something was hope, faith and a sense of purpose. I knew that I could do the job "IF" I just had the chance.

I knew that I could learn the job, "IF" I just had the opportunity. My faith, the love for my wife, the dream to do more and be better prevailed over my fear. I had faith and I took action.

I showed up at the corporate offices of the telecom company to find several hundred people waiting in multiple lines to interview with the leadership team. I managed to strategically maneuver to a shorter line.

As time progressed, it was finally my turn. I sat down and I hit the jack pot.... I was interviewing with the VP of sales! He reasonably pointed out that I didn't have a college degree. I said yes, that is true, but if he was willing to give me a chance, I would be his top salesperson. He laughed and we talked for a while. He then told me how he used to coach college football and how periodically they would have "walk-ons" come out for the team. These were individuals who did not have formal college football experience, but they usually had a strong desire and talent. He went on to say that sometimes he would meet a "walk-on" that had that special something. When he met those type of people, he was willing to give them a chance.

He said that he saw that same special something in me and that he was willing to give me a chance. I was in.

My faith and action had prevailed and would allow me to start my new life's journey! Because I had prayed and listened, I had overcome my fear, my doubt and my uncertainty. I had allowed God to put me in a position to fulfill my potential and to guide my direction. Later on in my life I would realize that taking that one small step allowed God to open more doors to larger opportunities. They would eventually lead me to become a vice president of sales for another telecom company years later and then onto my speaking career. All were stepping stones.

When you listen to what God is saying, by providing you with signs through what's working and what isn't, you can hear Him clearly enough.
You will feel it and you will know.

Where Are You Going?

God is our great navigator and we must believe that He will get us where we need to go, in His way and in His time. Even knowing this, most of us still work very hard at rerouting our lives to paths and destinations that we want to go, that look and feel familiar to us, or that we just want to pursue. This, by the way, is how we encounter more issues. Most of the time, you will find that we are the ones who get in the way of ourselves and in the way of God's work.

When you learn to focus on Him, you start to understand who He is and who He isn't.

When you figure this out, you can gain your life's focus and start understanding your purpose or your WHY.

When that moment happened for me, I decided to get my life headed in the right direction and to listen to His guidance.

27

Shortly afterwards, really amazing things started to happen. I'd like to think I'm a smart guy, but we undoubtedly know who we can give credit to for acts of miracles and "alignment of direction with opportunity." Some people call it luck, but we know better. Only the "Divine Maker of All" can bring miraculous intervention and guidance.

God is always there for us, but how can we hear or even know what He is saying if we aren't listening?

Here is a great way to start:
When you live your life in a way that honors God, you feel peace, His calling for you and you understand that your life is actually His life, as a gift to you. You start to see right from wrong.

He pulls you like a magnet and it is unmistakable.

Therefore one of the major and critical components to uncovering your WHY, to understand your purpose, starts with knowing who you are and where you are going. How are you living each day, and are you paying attention to how you are walking with Christ?

Thoughts, Actions and Words

Just as you measure miles if you are driving or you might measure dollars if you are saving money, you must measure your personal progress each and every day of your life. You measure yourself by being aware of your thoughts, your actions and your words. These are three very powerful tools that God has given us to use and act on through our own free will. We have the power to choose how we use them, therefore we must be responsible.

These gifts can be used for good and to benefit yourself and others, or they can be used negatively; sometimes hurting ourselves or others. You must constantly check how you are using your words, actions and thoughts and make modifications to ensure that they are used in ways that honor you and Him.

How you talk, think and behave are certainly your own choice, but that is precisely the point.

Since God has given us a choice and a life, His expectation is for us to value the freedom of these gifts for purposes of proper and higher value. Be aware of yourself when you are interacting with people. With others, if you become upset or emotional, you are more likely to think, do or say something that is not a true representation of who you are and what you think.

Also, be careful of your thoughts and actions when you are alone. A big challenge with being alone is that you might not feel accountability for your actions. It is easier to make an error in judgment when you feel you have no accountability. This is a false mindset that can and will deceive you.

God is always with you. Don't think of God as your monitor, think of Him as your protector. He has your best interest in mind even when you don't want Him to. It might seem uncomfortable at first and that is ok. Anything worthwhile in life will always take time and will always require hard work.

For example, if you are out of shape physically, you must take action to discipline yourself on a daily basis as you recondition your body. You didn't get out of shape overnight. The pain of neglect of many years will require much effort to reverse the negative effects on your body. It takes time and effort to get the results you want.

Likewise, if you have a weak area with your thoughts, words or actions, don't expect to change overnight. You can eventually change, however you must make the 'decision' to change yourself immediately. I do caution you to be reasonable with yourself and have patience as you start your new path towards success. Be your own encourager and seek encouragement from your supporters.

"Anything worthwhile in life will always take time and will always require hard work."

Comparing Yourself to Others.

"Success is not measured by what we do compared to what others do, success is measured by what you do with the abilities that God gave YOU." - *Zig Ziglar*

I need to point out to you that reading or hearing about other people improving their lives can sometimes make accomplishment appear easy. Let me assure you that nothing you or anyone else will go through to improve, will ever be easy. It never is.

In fact you know you are on the road to success when it is all uphill!

All of us are capable of doing or achieving great things. So the right question would be: Why don't we?
Think about this as it relates to YOUR life. You see, this is another big challenge that we face. We have a tendency to look outside of our lives at the accomplishments and success of others as a method of measurement with our own lives.

With social media today, it's easy to get a false impression of someone else's life when you read, see and hear things. Your mind is a powerful tool. If you let it, your imagination can and will create any circumstance that you are looking for, good or bad. This might affect how you view your current situation. After viewing posts that have been authored by others, we might get a false sense of who we think they are, what they have, what they do or what they have accomplished. Then, we use the perceived life status of others as a measurement tool of where our life is, and mistakenly compare it against how well we are doing.

Sometimes we even equate these perceived measurements of other's happiness and compare them against our own happiness. This is a big mistake and will ultimately lead you to disappointment. How silly is it to compare your own life with that of other people?

Everyone has challenges, issues and secrets, but most people don't broadcast their baggage to the world. Why would they? Most only show what they want the world to see. They paint the best possible picture.

"Your mind has a funny way of always finding what it is looking for."

When you consider t
very different than tha
conclude that you s
experiences of other p

God is preparing you
own purpose. You
challenges, disappoin
and successes. Looki
strengths, while being

CHAPTER 2 – Y

The Pain of Change

I have met many
type of unhap
most of th
are tra
eve

own weaknesses, is about as silly as an elephant admiring a hippo, while being disappointed in his own trunk. Although they may look similar, hippos and elephants are obviously two different animals, each given unique tools to allow them to function, excel and survive!

An elephant's trunk is valuable and necessary. However, if the elephant chooses to see it as ugly and unnecessary, then that is exactly what it will become.

As people, although we all look very similar, each of us has been given different tools that are unique to us and necessary for our own walk. The difference is that our tools are also found on the inside. If your mind does not see your tools (talents, desires and abilities) for what they are, then you will not see value in them. As a result, you will not use them. They will become worthless to you, even though they are still very valuable indeed.

people who at some point indicated some
ppiness in their lives. It always amazes me that
ese people have convinced themselves that they
pped in their own circumstances. They might have
become numb to their own pain and believe that
hange is too difficult or is not even an option. If you
introduced a bad habit, person or situation in your life, then
you can remove it!

If you have had a horrible event that has happened in your
life, it will certainly be upsetting, and you must allow
yourself time to grieve. However, at some point you must
choose to move on from the pain. You must find strength
to start moving forward again. Just as you are
subconsciously choosing to focus on the "event" that
happened in your life, you are also allowing pain to become
a part of who you are. This will inevitably hold you down
and hold you back. Choose to be alive and to live with
purpose!

*"If you introduced a bad habit,
person or situation into your life,
then you can remove it!"*

I used to drink with my corporate sales buddies. I never thought twice about it. Eventually though, I started to notice that drinking was affecting my life personally, professionally and spiritually. It was also affecting my health. The after effects had become very painful in my life. I knew I needed to stop, but when I considered stopping, it was more painful to give up the "perceived benefits" of drinking and socializing, than it was to endure the pain of quitting. So, of course I didn't stop. My realization to stop only came when I was given a wake-up call one evening after a corporate happy hour. That night would prove to be a turning point in my life.

If you have ever experienced someone who is inebriated, then you know that your mind does not function properly. It is impossible to sober up quickly. Well that was me. Bonnie had escorted me to our room, where I immediately fell to sleep.

Suddenly, I was in a very large, endless area with hundreds of people. It was calm and very quiet. We were all standing in a line that zig-zagged back and forth for what looked like miles. I wasn't afraid, I was just curious to know where I was and what was happening. I looked at the faces of the others around me in line. No one was talking and most had anxious or looks of deep thought on their faces. The line slowly kept moving.

As I looked forward, I noticed that everyone was passing through an archway made of fire; it was blowing flames on them as they walked through. Immediately, I considered that I might be in hell! That thought was quickly interrupted by my confirmation that I was saved and that hell wasn't an option. Suddenly, I was walking directly through the archway. It blew fire on me, but nothing happened; it didn't burn or hurt me. I realized right then, that the fire was there to show me that I was not in my body. In this very real experience, I was dead! That is when it hit me with complete clarity. Everyone, including me, was in line waiting for our judgment.

The line kept moving. It didn't stop and you couldn't leave. You had to keep going. I finally understood the solemn and anxious faces. Right then, I heard Him talk to me. He said, "Michael, you will come to see me one day. It will happen. Will you be prepared when you come before me?" I wasn't concerned before, but now ……..

(Note: Years later, I was sharing this story with my new friend Hanna. She pointed out to me that the fire archway was actually from scripture. I had no idea: 1st Corinthians 3:13-15 **"their work will be shown for what it is, because the Day will bring it to light. It will be revealed with fire, and the fire will test the quality of each person's work. [14]If what has been built survives, the builder will receive a reward. [15] If it is burned up, the builder will suffer loss but yet will be saved—even though only as one escaping through the flames."**)

Suddenly I sat straight up. I was in my bed and surprisingly, I was wide awake. I had so many emotions going through my mind. I quickly leaned over to wake up Bonnie, but to my surprise, she was already awake. She looked surprised to see me up and alert. She was lying on the bed next to me, with her arm and hand propping up her head.

I said "Bonnie, you are not going to believe what just happened to me. I had this alarming dream, it was so real!" I then proceeded to tell her the details.

When I finished, she just started crying. I asked her what was wrong. She told me when I came home, she was very worried about me. She said that while I was sleeping, she started praying over me. She had asked God to help me, to speak to me and to fill me with conviction. I held her and started crying. It was divine intervention. Not only did He answer Bonnie's prayer that night, He also answered mine long term. My days of feeling terrible physically, mentally and spiritually and portraying myself in a way that would compromise my faith, were over.

The pain of my situation had become greater than the pain of taking action to make change in my life, so I took action to change. I removed alcohol from my life completely.

I had hope, I prayed, I believed and I took decisive action. I didn't try to quit, I DID quit and I made a commitment to follow through every day.

I'm not encouraging you to stop drinking, that's your own decision. However, I do want you to think about any pains in your life.

Do you have pains that have become greater than the pain of taking action to change?
Is it time for you to take action to change?
Is God talking to you about something?
You have the power to act on it through His strength!

Pains can and will come in different forms throughout your life. You must identify what you (or others close to you) can and cannot live with. Then make a decision, humble yourself and take immediate action to change.

"When the pain of your current situation becomes greater than the pain of taking action, you must take action to resolve the pain."

POSITIVE AFFIRMATIONS:

- ➢ God is always here with me.
- ➢ He is guiding my path for His plans for me.
- ➢ I will enjoy quiet time and listen to what He is revealing to me each day.
- ➢ I will choose to use my words, actions and thoughts wisely.
- ➢ I will not compare myself to others, as my life is mine.
- ➢ I have talents, desires and abilities that are unique to me.
- ➢ I will identify pains in my life.
- ➢ I will take action to resolve those pains.

CHAPTER 3 – Your VALUE

Chapter 3

Your Value

"As long as you are breathing, your life has value."

- Mike Rodriguez

CHAPTER 3 – Your VALUE

I don't know what you have been through in your life, but I do know this: Everyone will experience challenges and everyone will experience successes in their life. The determining factor of any outcome is in fact YOU and the decision that you make, or don't make, to keep moving forward. You have the ability to change your mind-set about who you are and what you are going to do about your life. Happiness is a choice and carrying around your past is also a choice. You can become a victim or a victor!

I want you to think of this, and say it to yourself whenever you are feeling low: "I have value. As long as I am breathing, my life has value."
How do I know? Because you are alive!

Your life is a gift that was given to you for a reason.
Because it is a gift to you, you must believe that you are strong enough to live it. There is a difference between being alive and living your life. Let's start with being alive:

Being alive is a gift that is validated by your breathing, so if you are breathing, then you are alive. Breathing is a miracle that only God can effortlessly give. You do not have a choice in the matter of breathing. Yes, you can make your own breathing stop, but by doing this you would directly take away the divine gift of life that you have been given. Therefore, God gives life to us and He allows us to be alive.

So if you are breathing, then we can conclude that you have a purpose. However, it is possible to be alive and not be living your life towards your purpose.

Living, on the other hand, is based on a few things: Your faith in your creator, your belief in your purpose and value, your decision to think, speak and act on that purpose, and your actions to positively impact each and every day through your desires. Your attitude towards all of this will align your thoughts, words and actions, directly to the quality of your life. You must work at living!

When you choose to live your life, it means that you understand that failure is an event, that although something may have happened to you, that "it" does not define you. You believe that you can and will move forward, because you have a purpose, so you do. You empower yourself through God's love. You remind yourself that taking daily action to pursue something in your life that will make you better, will make others better.

You understand that living is a choice and you pursue a quality life. You find your own joy.

You may come from a family or work at a job where they do not see your value. You may be in a relationship where a person does not see your value.

Just because someone else fails to see your worth does not mean that you do not have any worth. Never let someone else define who you are. Make a claim to yourself that as long as you are breathing and living that you have value.

How Do You View Yourself?

Do you recognize that because you are breathing that you are alive and because you are alive that you have value?
Can you see the potential and value that you have?
What are the skills or talents that you have and enjoy?
Do you focus on your strengths or your weaknesses?

Consider this: What if you were to make, draw or paint a picture? After you were done with your creation, you were so proud of your work that you proudly displayed it on a wall in your home. To you, it was unique and it was beautiful, because it was yours; you were the one who made it! Now what if someone came to your house, saw the painting and criticized it! What if they even pulled it off of the wall, said it was worthless and stuck it in your closet?

Your life is the same as this example. We are a work of art from our Father. We are His creation, made in His image with love and passion! When we criticize ourselves, we are criticizing His work!

When we don't use the talents and abilities that were given to us, it is just like taking the art off the wall and putting it in a closet. No one can see it, use it or get the benefit of it.

We hang art on a wall proudly for everyone to see. God gives us life and our talents the same way, to display and use for a purpose in this world! We are magnificent and we know this is true because we are alive and being displayed for the world to see!

Do not criticize yourself!
Do not accept negative criticism from others, because they are only challenging the awesome work of our God! He is the creator of the universe and He does not make mistakes. You are who you are because you were created that way. He needs to use you to fill a need in this world with the uniqueness that you were given. View yourself as a priceless work of art that is being displayed to the world for God's purposes on this earth.

View yourself as valuable, because you are.
View yourself as beautiful, because you are.
View yourself as smart, because you are.
View yourself as happy, because you should be.
View yourself as strong, because you are.
View yourself as a work of art, because you are.
View yourself how you want to be….. And you will be.

As you confess God's truth about your life, you will start to see, you will start to believe and more importantly, you will start to become. You will start to recognize the beauty, value and desires that you were born with that have always been inside of you. You must believe that you, your life and your talents are all gifts from God.

A Unique Seed

The Chinese Bamboo tree is unique and grows from a very tiny seed. Most people who see the seed, do not know or understand the value and potential of the seed. They simply see it as a small seed. However, much like us, these seeds are indeed special. When they are planted, they must be watered and cared for daily. If you stop caring for the tiny seed at any time while it is underground, it will stop growing and it will die.

However, if you make time to care for the seed and if you choose to take action to feed and water it each day, something amazing will happen. The seed will slowly start to grow. Unlike most seeds, however, the Chinese Bamboo tree takes 5 long years before it breaks ground. Why? Because beneath the ground it is growing a foundational system of roots.

These deep roots will support a sprout that is strong enough to break through the ground. It requires discipline, work and faith to ensure that this small seed will develop into a small sprout.

After 5 long years, the little sprout will start to break through the soil, but this isn't the amazing part. After it breaks through the dirt, within weeks the once small sprout will forcefully and quickly start to grow into its purpose: a Chinese Bamboo tree. After 5 weeks these trees can reach up to 90 feet tall, becoming some of the tallest trees in the world. The question is, does the Chinese Bamboo tree grow in 5 weeks or in 5 years? The answer is 5 years.

Our lives are much like the Chinese Bamboo tree. We spend our life growing and preparing our foundations, as we work.

Our roots are developing and strengthening to support the magnificent growth that is coming! Like the Chinese Bamboo tree, our purpose does not happen overnight. Sometimes it can take many years. We must be patient and we must have faith, until one day, when our foundation is strong enough, we will break through and grow into our full potential. When it comes it will be amazing!

Always Have Hope

In your own life, things may not be happening in the time frame that you want or need them to happen. If you are at a similar point in your life, where you are working and not seeing progress, I want to let you know that you must have hope. Hope is the internal belief that things can and, most importantly, will be better. Without hope, you will ultimately resign yourself to accept your current situation. Acceptance will then cause you and your circumstances to appear hopeless. This can become overwhelming and very difficult to change, but you can do it.

You must identify the challenges in your life. This will require deep thought, honesty, accountability and time.

Let's say that you are unemployed and you have identified that your challenge is that you cannot get a job.

Then, when we look closer, we uncover that your confidence and belief about whether you will even get a new job is actually very low. You may have emailed or posted your resume to many employers with no response. Because of this, your attitude about the competition and the job marketplace is such that you actually wonder if you will ever even get a job. Your hope is now being compromised! As a result, you may not give all that you are capable of, and your efforts probably won't be in line with your potential.

In this scenario, your challenge may not be that you can't get a job. It may be your own lack of hope about the outcome of "not" getting a job that is actually the real challenge. You might be getting in your own way.

If we were to dig deeper into this situation, we might learn that your problem could be influenced by three factors:

1. Your attitude about your ability to even get a job,
2. Your reduced efforts based on your attitude, and
3. Your lack of strategy to get a job.

Ironically, all of these are critically influenced by hope.

By changing your attitude and believing that the right job is indeed out there for you, by default you will improve your efforts, your performance and your results!

Then, by having a new attitude and a clear viewpoint, you can change your strategy to find a new job. You might call employers directly, network live with friends and start reaching out to contacts on social media. By taking these new steps, you will increase your chances of getting a job.

Always believe and always have hope. Evaluate what you are thinking, doing and saying and make adjustments to keep yourself on track.

Taking Care of Yourself

You must work to maintain everything that you care about. We have determined that since you are breathing, you are alive. This means that God cares about you and you have value. You understand that you have a purpose and since you are living, you have a responsibility to fill that purpose.

It is difficult to accomplish most feats even when you are healthy, happy and spiritually sound. It is more challenging when you are sick, unhappy or lacking faith. When you are in very poor health, or depressed, things are usually perceived as impossible and will probably not get done at all. This is especially true if you are keeping God out of your life. Anything worthwhile requires effort. If you maintain your car and your home, they will last longer. The same goes for your body, mind and faith. To keep balance in your life, you must make an effort every day.

Physically – Our bodies are amazing and resilient. As you exercise, your body starts adapting and improving. It starts strengthening your muscles and starts burning the unhealthy fat. You must be the catalyst that starts the process. As your body gets healthier, so does your immunity, your energy and your ability to take action. This means less sick time, better sleep, more energy and more productivity!

Mentally – Our minds are the command center of our body. How you think is how you act and speak. What you put into your mind determines who you are and who you will become. You do this by reading, praying and putting good things in your mind. Your words are expressions of your thoughts. Keep your mind sharp and clear and your thoughts will be sharp and clear to keep you aware. You must be in tune with your spiritual desires and passions.

Spiritually – You must take care of yourself spiritually, with the same discipline and passion that we do with our mind and body. Pray, relax, study scripture and go to church. Your spirituality requires the same time and energy as your physical and mental health. It is the core of who you are. In time, it will reveal what you are called to do. Your spirituality helps you to keep your balance.

I was overweight for many years. Because I chose to let myself carry excessive and unnecessary weight, I received all of the problems that came with abusing my body. I had high blood pressure and I was on cholesterol medicine. When I finally decided to take action and take control over the kind of food that I chose to put in my mouth, things started to change. As I started to put healthier food in my mouth, my body had to start adapting. Over the course of a year, I lost an enormous 45 pounds! I became healthier and was also able to get off of those medications!

Likewise, you must manage your spiritual and mental well-being. Read and listen to good stuff and think positive and powerful thoughts to keep your mind sharp. Get into a good church and practice your faith daily, not just on Sunday. Read your Bible, a Bible app or find scriptures on-line that you can relate to. Hang around other people who share the same faith and values as you do.

You may not currently be in the shape that you want to be in any of the 3 categories previously listed, however you must claim your success and your future! You must recondition your mind to act, think and speak for where you expect to be, not for where you are!
You can do it!

Act, think and speak for where you expect to be, not for where you are!

Being Alone / Being Lonely

I moved out of my parent's house when I was way too young. I remember the first night of being on my own. It was nothing like I expected. I was alone AND I was lonely.

Most college freshman can relate to this. When you leave the comfort of something familiar, it is uncomfortable and therefore you feel the pain. However, there is a big difference between being alone and being lonely.

As you grow in your faith, you find that being alone isn't so bad, because you learn to understand that you really are not alone. You can use your thoughts to pray, think and find peace in the silence of your own mind. You start to enjoy the silence and you start enjoying who you are.

In order to get what I am saying, you must fully understand and accept what loneliness is. Ready? Here it is: Loneliness is a feeling. It is YOUR OWN feeling.

According to Wikipedia: **Loneliness** *is a complex and usually unpleasant emotional response to isolation or lack of companionship.*

Did you catch that? It is an emotional response! Meaning, that you can control it. The reason we are lonely is because we are looking on the outside of who we are, to find something or someone who can fill or remove that unpleasant emotion that we are feeling on the inside.

It is only when we start looking on the inside and recognize who we are, and whose we are, that we understand we are never truly alone.

Just as we might choose to feel sad and alone, we can also choose to do other positive things and enjoy who we are. Take a walk, ride a bike, read a book, or just relax and think. We can choose to tap into the company of our own thoughts and feelings or of the companionship of the Lord.

This is where mental health and confidence can come in. As you see yourself in a positive way and you have faith, you start to have peace. Learn to like yourself and enjoy time with you! The end result?.....

"Just because you are alone, doesn't mean that you have to be lonely."

You do not and should not have to rely on other people and/or things to give you a sense of good feeling or sense of comfort. Let me clarify that people and things can help to create a sense of happiness, but we should not become dependent on them for our personal happiness.

Besides your spiritual relationship with our Lord, the best relationship you can have is with yourself. Before you can truly give love to others, you must have lots of love to give. Get to know yourself and enjoy who you are! Love yourself, unconditionally, so you can learn to love unconditionally.

POSITIVE AFFIRMATIONS:

- ➢ As long as I am breathing, my life has value.
- ➢ I will focus on my strengths.
- ➢ I will view myself as strong, because I am.
- ➢ I will view myself as beautiful, because I am.
- ➢ I will view myself as smart, because I am.
- ➢ I will view myself as capable, because I am.
- ➢ I will view myself as happy, because I am.
- ➢ Regardless of my situation, I will always keep hope. Things will always get better.
- ➢ I will work each day to keep myself healthy: spiritually, mentally and physically.
- ➢ I choose not to feel lonely, even when I am alone.
- ➢ I love myself unconditionally, so I can learn to love others unconditionally.

Chapter 4

Your Purpose

"..and he will tell you
what is yet to come."
-    John 16:3

CHAPTER 4 – Your PURPOSE

CHAPTER 4 – Your PURPOSE

God has a plan for your life. Sometimes that plan may not go the way you want it to go or even need it to go. You must understand and accept that it will serve a purpose when it is time, according to His will and according to His time.

HE Works in Mysterious Ways

A few months after I had decided to remove alcohol from my life, I was working with a very prominent telecom company. I was based in Dallas, Texas and my job was to fly around the U.S., working with various strategic partners, providing them with business assistance and expertise.

One day I received an urgent call from one of our partners in Charlotte, North Carolina, who was in a bad position. He had a meeting with a local hospital and he required my assistance at that meeting. He informed me that the meeting he needed me to attend was only a week away and I would need to book a flight immediately. I really didn't want to go, because I knew that with such short notice, I would almost definitely have to book a connecting flight. This would cause a lot of waiting and also create a risk for flight delays. It boiled down to a lot of hassle for me.

59

After trying to figure a way out of going, I finally resigned myself to the fact that I was needed and that I should go, so I did. I attended the meeting and, as it turned out, we finished early. I was happy because I could now get to the airport and catch an early flight back. It all worked out like clockwork, except that I had to really hustle to get on the earlier flight.

When I arrived, they were already boarding, but I made it. As I approached the gate, I heard someone call my name. I was startled and looked up to see my brother's friend Steve who also lived in Frisco. What a surprise encounter! I asked what he was doing in Charlotte and he explained that he too happened to be in town on business. I let him know that I was lucky to have caught this flight, otherwise I would still be waiting in the airport a few more hours for my original flight. We boarded the plane, I grabbed my seat and Steve walked back to his. What a coincidence to see a familiar face in a city far across the U.S., I thought.

A few minutes into the flight Steve approached me and asked to sit with me. I said of course, as I was happy to have some company. I also like Steve. He asked me if I wanted a drink and I let him know that I had made a decision to removed drinking from my life. We talked the entire flight from Charlotte to Dallas. (Well, I talked and Steve drank).

At the end of the flight we said our goodbyes and agreed that we should keep in touch. Now I need you to understand that prior to that flight, I had only seen and/or talked with Steve a few times.

Now, fast-forward a few years later, after our unique encounter on that plane in another city. I was reaching out to people to join a new online group I had started. A few weeks later, I received a text from Steve. He wanted to meet me for lunch. How cool! I agreed and we met a few days later.

When I saw him, he reached down to give me a great big bear hug. Steve is a big man with an even bigger heart.

As we sat down, Steve asked me if I remembered that flight from Charlotte a few years earlier. I told him that I did. Steve said that he wanted to let me know that our in-depth conversation about removing alcohol from my life had stuck with him. He told me that although it took him a year or so after that encounter, that he too was working to become stronger in his walk and that he had evaluated drinking in his own life.

He then shared with me how he had become closer with God and how God was working through him. Steve said he was very active in his church and was even helping to open new churches!

I always thought it was a great act of God that I was able to connect with Steve that day, in that city out of anywhere else or with anyone else. Especially since I was supposed to be on another flight.

Now you can look back on this story and say well Mike, that is really cool, but it's just a coincidence. I would respond by saying that's my point: with God there is never coincidence. God always has plans. Although we may not understand His plans from our mind or our viewpoint, He is always working in our lives in His way. This is exactly what He did with both me and my friend Steve Flad.

You see God used our encounter as a vessel to plant a seed of faith that would growing over a period of time. Neither one of us knew it was happening. In fact, God's plan had started well before both of us were aware, by putting us in a sudden situation to meet and talk, all the way across the country. God had created an urgent situation in my business, caused a meeting to end earlier than expected, changed travel plans and even coordinated our flight together, all for His purpose to touch and reinforce our individual life plans.

That trip helped to remind me that God is always in control and preparing people and situations today, for His plans tomorrow, and years to come.

God will put the right people, situations and circumstances in your life to work His will. However, there really is no such thing as a coincidence.

What About All of These Problems?

Problems will happen and will certainly be defined differently to each person. What might be a small issue to someone else, can be considered devastating to you. Either way, going through problems are God's way of strengthening us to become better and stronger.

A muscle can only grow and strengthen if it is worked hard and pushed to its capacity. When a muscle is worked out with heavy weights, the muscle tissue is actually being destroyed and broken down. Then, after much rest and agony to the weightlifter, the muscle will start to build over the damaged tissue to repair itself.

By going through this process over and over again, the muscle becomes larger, stronger and starts to take shape.

This same process applies to us as we go through life's challenges. We become broken down and we go through agony as we start a similar growth process.

Because of the pain of the situation, most of us will try to avoid and go around life's problems. The way we are made, we must go through problems in order to grow. We do this to follow God's will and plan for our life. You must look at any problem you are facing as an opportunity that serves a purpose. You may not understand the purpose today, but it can be very relevant and helpful when you are facing another of life's challenges in the future. Challenges and problems will come in all shapes and sizes.

When my daughter Lauren was in high school, she was applying to colleges. There was a delay in hearing back from the schools that she wanted to attend, and she started worrying about even getting accepted. Lauren always performed well academically, so I knew there wasn't an issue with her getting in a good school. Even still, she worried. After many prayers and calming conversations, the offer letters started flowing in.

Lauren was really leaning towards SMU, Baylor, and TCU. As it turned out, Baylor was the first to respond with the good news, and then acceptance came from the others. Baylor stood out, not only because they offered her a nice partial scholarship, but also they pursued her with genuine interest. After a visit to the campus, Lauren (and our family) were 100% convinced that Baylor was where she should be. We had prayed and we felt it. There was only one problem.

The balance for the tuition was WAY more than I wanted to pay. I could afford it, just didn't want to pay it. Lauren's prayer had been answered, but now I was faced with what I thought was a problem. I could have easily said 'no' and asked her to go to a cheaper school, but I had been the one to tell her to have no limits, to trust God, because He always has a plan. Now here I was, questioning my own words. I thought I was stuck, so I prayed. Almost immediately, I felt God tell me that He put Lauren where she needed to be; that He gave me the resources and now it was time to do my part and pay.

I didn't have a problem. I was just being selfish. You see years before, God had positioned me financially to be able to provide the tuition. I heeded his calling, told Lauren she was now a Baylor Bear, and I happily paid the tuition. Only two months later, I was blessed with a new job and a substantial financial bonus. I would have felt really silly had I doubted our God. I realize now that God wanted me to accept that situation as a testament of his capabilities, to always trust in Him. He will provide what you need for the path and purpose that He has laid out for you.

After Lauren was settled into Baylor, she felt at home as she acclimated to her new environment. She found she struggled with balancing her new responsibilities of studying and social life.

At the end of her first semester, she realized that her grades had suffered. Now she had a problem.

Lauren came home for Christmas, feeling sad and concerned as she explained her situation to us. Her GPA had dropped below the standard for keeping her scholarship. She would have to substantially increase her GPA to even get to the minimum to keep her scholarship and stay at Baylor. She said that the increase was going to be extremely hard. I explained to her that nothing is impossible if it is God's will. I shared with her that she could do it, as long as she believed that she could, and as long as she had made the commitment to make it happen.

I reminded her that she was already where she was supposed to be. God had already shown her by making it possible for her to get into Baylor.

Lauren had made the commitment, she had taken action and she had studied like never before, learning to say "no" to friends when she needed to and trusting God that the work would pay off.

We prayed hard and waited. When her new grades came out, not only had she attained the GPA that she thought was very difficult, but she had actually exceeded it! All was well again. It had always been well with God.

Lauren, like me, never had a problem. She had a wake-up call. This event reminded her of her purpose, her identity, and of her gift. She was pushed to her capacity to trust in God and to use her God-given potential. She realized she had placed a lot of her self-worth in where she was going to school, and in almost losing Baylor, she learned to redirect her identity in the Lord, and not in a University or in her GPA. He used that situation to show her that she was capable, and that with Him, anything is possible.

Everyone's problems are all relative, but we all can agree that losing someone close to you can be life altering.

In early 2013, Bonnie's mother, Sharon Malmer, suddenly became seriously ill and was admitted to the hospital. Sharon had been to the hospital in the past a few times for various reasons, so we just assumed that she would be in and out as usual.

We were right and after a few days, she was released. The family went to see her at the recovery clinic to see how she was doing. We walked in to find her sitting in a chair watching a little bird right outside of her window. She turned as she noticed us and gave us her kind and warm smile. She was very happy to see us and we were equally happy to see her. We spent quality time with her and I asked her to get better, because we needed her around. However, this encounter would be different for all of us.

That same night we received a call that Sharon was admitted into ICU. She suddenly had turned for the worse. After several days of being on life-support, it was apparent that she was not going to make it.

On March 3, 2013, on her 51st wedding anniversary to Bill Malmer; Sharon Malmer left us to go be with our Lord.

No one was prepared for Sharon's death. There was an overwhelming sadness and grief that blanketed all of our lives. Sharon was a kind woman with a generous and caring heart. She always had a smile and nice words to share with everyone she talked to. She loved the Lord and showed that love through her actions. I immediately started to realize that Bonnie's grief was overwhelming. She was very close with her mother and the reality of Sharon's death was setting in.

I knew that I had to be strong for Bonnie, and I knew that I needed to trust in God for that strength. I started praying more often and longer.

As I look back over the loss of such an amazingly wonderful person, I can know that God's plan was always in place. Sharon had been sick on and off and I believe that she was ready to go to heaven. Losing Sharon made me look at life differently.

Through this major life's problem, I started to see a whole new love for my wife Bonnie and a new appreciation for my own life. I could see all of the gifts that Sharon had left for us through being Bonnie's mother. Bonnie is also kind, unselfish and loving and she is now passing that gift onto our girls.

I started to understand how valuable life is and how precious the time is that we are given. This event gave me the grace to look at life from a different perspective; to maximize my potential while on this earth.

We will always miss Sharon. I think of her often, and I usually start crying, thinking that she is no longer here. That sadness is always followed by a smile and a comforting feeling in my heart as I remember her. Her passing helped me to become more aware of my love for others.

One night, shortly after she was gone, I was praying and I felt God telling me that Sharon was safe with him. In my mind I could hear her say, "Oh wow, it's so beautiful." I know that was real; I know where she is and I know that she is safe and healthy now. Most importantly, I know that we will see her again.

Everything happens for a reason. Go through your problems and face them head-on, knowing that God is with you! Every situation in life is temporary.

Trust in Him, grow and you will become stronger. He will turn something great out of every problem that you face.

Having Peace through Faith

Faith is the ability to trust completely, even when it seems unreasonable. Through my own problems, God has given me a strong awareness of His presence. Through this, I have been able to know, not think, that He has been in control of my life. He provides guidance to all of us, if we will only slow down to connect with Him. God communicates to each of us differently, but I am convinced that He does communicate with us.

In my early twenties, before I moved to Dallas and met Bonnie, I had moved to Austin in an attempt to improve myself. I found that even though I had moved, changed my environment, my friends and my residence; I was still the same. After a while, the same problems that I had previously, started to show up again. I was young and stubborn and wasn't willing to listen to anyone. Blaming was a big part of my life and I was convinced that I was a victim and everyone else was the issue.

My recklessness kept me from connecting with God.

One day after another disappointing situation, I was driving down a long road. I was at a very low point in my life. I was broke, living with my sister and working for my brother-in-law as a house painter. I had no friends, I was miserable and I felt worthless. I knew that I could do better and that I was called to do better.

I remember that my complete feeling was that God had let me down and had left me. I was furious with Him and felt abandoned and lost. How could He let me get to this horrible place?
Why did He let this happen?
Why wasn't He answering my prayers!
I was overwhelmed with anger and emotion and I lost it.
I started crying, shouting at and cursing Him, "Why would you let this happen to me, I thought you were supposed to be here for me! I trusted you and you have abandoned me. You probably don't even exist," followed by "Why don't you ever answer me?" And then, one final time I yelled as loud as I could, with so much contempt, with such a sorrowful heart and with my eyes full of tears, "Why don't you ever show yourself to me!?"

I don't remember much after that, but this is what I do remember. The sky quickly opened from the ground, all the way up to the clouds, and then it shut in a flash. It shut just as quickly as it had opened. It all happened in what was faster than the blink of a human eye.

In that instant, I felt an amazing power that was tremendously overwhelming. I knew it was God. He had revealed a tiny flash of His presence to me.

Then He spoke to me. To this day I don't know why, but He did. He said, "Michael I am here, I am with you and I have always been with you, but I am too much for you to even understand. You could not handle my full presence. I am everything and I am in everything around you. I am in the trees and in every leaf, I am in the air and in the clouds in the sky. I am in every blade of grass, in the sun and the stars. I have been with you and I will always be with you."

I was in awe and I was in shock. I couldn't drive and I had to pull over immediately. I stopped my car on the side of the road and with tears running down my face, I just started praying and saying that I was sorry…so sorry. I wasn't afraid, but I had been set straight. I was shocked, humbled, embarrassed, comforted and at peace, all at the same time. I thanked Him for that miracle of a split second, and that was the last time that I would ever challenge God in my life. God does work in His own way and in His own time. I don't know if He will ever do that same thing for you, because God is after all… God.

What I learned that day is that God is bigger than anything that I could ever imagine. He "IS" everything and He is in everything, because He created it.

He truly is in control, without a doubt. This is why He calls Himself "I am." That experience strengthened my faith even more.

When we get to the point where we know that God does indeed exist and we also accept that He is who He says He is, faith becomes the next thing that we must strengthen. Faith is trusting that God is in control of every circumstance in your life. When we gain that depth of understanding, then with clarity we understand things might not go the way we think they will go or how we even want them to go. That doesn't mean the end result won't be the same.

So if God really is in control, and we are living our life the right way and doing the right things, according to His will, then consider this: We have absolutely nothing to worry about. The absence of worry creates peace.

Therefore, faith equals peace and love.

"Faith is trusting that God is in control of every circumstance in your life."

When you can lie down to sleep at night peacefully, that is a testament to your faith.

When you can spend quality time with your spouse, children and friends without worry, then you are showing your Faith.

When you can enjoy where you are and who you are with, without any fear or worry, then you are truly living through Faith.

When you trust that tomorrow and all of the things that come with it are in God's hands, that is true faith.

"Therefore I tell you, do not worry about your life, what you will eat or drink; or about your body, what you will wear. Is not life more than food, and the body more than clothes?
Look at the birds of the air; they do not sow or reap or store away in barns, and yet your heavenly Father feeds them. Are you not much more valuable than they?
- Matthew 6:25

Trusting that God's plan and power is greater than any thought or circumstance that we can create or encounter, allows us to have a peaceful mind.
That kind of faith is the kind that the Bible tells us to have:

He Has Already Shown You

All of my life I have wanted to be in front of the crowd speaking with people, one way or another. That has been my desire. When I was a child, I was the class clown or the center of attention. As I got older, I always felt comfortable speaking, mentoring and talking with groups.

Had I learned to pay attention to the gifts that I have been given, and had I listened to how He was telling me to use them, I would have saved myself a bunch of trouble. It is the same for all of us. You weren't created to be born, work, eat and then pay bills, taxes and die. Those are requirements in life, but they may not be pushing you to your purpose.

It's kind of like your job. It is a requirement for you to show up for work, but that may not push you towards the purpose of your job or to excel. The reason you show up is for money. The purpose of your job is to fill your objectives in life, whatever they may be. You may want a bigger house, a promotion, a nicer car, a vacation, kids in college, etc.

In life, your purpose is about finding a need in this world and filling it based on God's plan. Every one of us has a certain skillset that is only relevant to us. This is why you can never compare yourself to anyone else.

Each person has a different purpose and as a result, a different and unique set of skills. I say unique because they are yours, given to you. I am convinced that these skills are manifested through our own pure desires. I believe that this is how we are shown.

As I started my professional speaking career, I did have doubts and "what if's." About that same time, one night I had a very vivid dream. I saw myself as a very young boy, watching someone speak to a group of children. I realized it was a real event from an earlier part of my life. In the dream, I could remember being so excited about that person talking to the group. I had such strong feelings to do exactly what they were doing...speaking with people!

God shared with me in that same dream these words: "Michael, I'm showing you this to let you know that this has always been in you. I put the desire to speak inside of you when I made you. It has always been a part of you."

In that dream, He revealed to me what we should all know and understand; that our purpose has been predefined. It is a part of you just like your eyes, your heart, your hair and your feelings. Just like your feelings, we can get confused and complicate things, when we do not follow the right path.

CHAPTER 4 – Your PURPOSE

The important thing to know is that He showed me that I didn't just imagine this whole idea of speaking. He showed me that I was letting my purpose develop in my life and that it had always been a part of me. It was a part of my life for His plans. If you listen, and keep your eyes and mind alert and obedient, you will see what He has already shown you.

After that dream it all made sense. He was right (of course). I now understand why the things in my life have happened the way they have. As I look back, I realize and can see the path that He has laid out for me. I can identify where I got off course. I can now clearly see that my passion was never being in corporate America, my passion was speaking with and helping people I met in corporate America. Corporate America, however was preparing me for my WHY.

The funny thing is, almost all of those people had at some point already told me what God knew all along, as if to remind me. Things like "Mike, you really should go into public speaking" and "Mike, you have a gift for speaking" and "Mike, why don't you consider speaking professionally." My favorites have always been "Mike, you missed your calling," "You should be a preacher or a motivational speaker" or "you should write a book."
It appears that they were seeing more than I was. This is why we need to stop, pray and listen. Deep down we always know what He is telling us, through what we have already been shown.

POSITIVE AFFIRMATIONS:

- ➤ I must trust that God has a plan for me, in his way and in his time.
- ➤ Problems are opportunities for me to learn and to become stronger.
- ➤ I will work to have peace through faith in all of my thoughts.
- ➤ I know that God has already shown me my desires, skills and talents that He has put in me.
- ➤ I do have a purpose and I will fulfill it.

Chapter 5

Taking Action

*"Through Faith and Action
All Things Are Possible."*
-   Mike Rodriguez

CHAPTER 5 – Taking ACTION

As you read through the different chapters in this book and evaluate your life and your life situation, you will start having an awareness or an awakening of things that have happened in your own life.

The knowledge of who you are and what you are capable of attaining is the first part of any journey. Then, as you continue to develop your confidence and faith, you will start to understand that you are indeed capable. This new confidence should prompt you to start setting goals and start seeking the paths to the opportunities that align you with where you need to go.

All of this will mean absolutely nothing to you, if you don't take action. As you live, you will primarily receive negative and positive influences from two sources:

1. Exterior sources: Friends, family, internet, etc.
2. Interior sources: What God fills you with, what you tell yourself and what you choose to believe.

Are YOU Your Biggest Obstacle?

"I could never do that, I'm not good enough, I can't do that".....and the list goes on.

We use words to express how we think and feel; so our words are indeed an expression of our thoughts. Words are very powerful. When you use words in a negative way, they can have devastating impact on the receiver. But what if WE are the receiver of our own negative words? You might say that is ridiculous.....and that is the issue. We do.

The limitations that we impose on ourselves and the confidence that we generate to succeed, are all a result of our own internal belief system of how we view who we are.

When you think self-defeating thoughts, you are actually conditioning your mind and teaching yourself how to believe, what to accept and how to respond to situations.
You are defining your very own self. Consider that what you confess with your words, has already been created as a thought that you have already accepted. Your mouth is simply using your own words to state what your brain already believes; what you have already told yourself.

The end result is this:
When you state that you "cannot do something" ...you won't.

When you say that you "aren't good at something" or that "you aren't good enough" you won't be, and when you say "that will never happen for me" it probably won't happen either. Why? Because you have already told yourself who you are and how you should respond. Your mind is simply acting on what you believe! When you say "I can't" or "I'm not good at" your mind and body will respond to this self-affirmation to the level that you believe. In this case, it will be at a very low level.

You can start increasing your chances for success, by simply making a decision to believe that you can be successful! Then start changing your words. Say the opposite of what you have been saying and use positive self-affirmations. It will be uncomfortable at first, but consider the benefits! You are being confident, not arrogant by feeding your mind and teaching it how to respond and improve your results!

When you tell yourself positive things, your mind will start to believe. When you use positive, confident and forward thinking words, you are reinforcing your own thoughts. Your mind will then create a new response system that will work to "find a way" and will push you to action!

I'm not saying that you will start immediately succeeding in all of your endeavors, but what I am saying is that you will significantly increase your chances of succeeding.

Zig Ziglar taught us that "You are what you are and you are where you are, because of what has gone into your mind. You can change what you are and you can change where you are, by changing what goes into your mind." This statement is the truth behind changing how you view yourself and if you will determine to move forward. Life is difficult enough, don't be your own obstacle. Confess success!

Through Faith and Action, All Things are possible

Faith demands attention when your weakness calls it. You must have faith and you must take action when a situation you are faced with is beyond your scope of strength. Your faith is the fuel that will prompt you to action. Action creates the steps that are needed to get you where you plan or need to go.

As you continue your journey and encounter failures and setbacks, your faith will empower you to get back up.

You must keep going and focus on your goals in a new and different light. When you regain your power and your confidence, you will take action again and again. By doing this, you will increase your chances to succeed.

If you have ever seen or experienced a sand storm, you know that it is a very frightening situation. As the cloud of sand engulfs the individual, their main senses are almost completely cut off. The person becomes disoriented, fear immediately takes over and escalates the situation very quickly. They cannot see, cannot hear and can barely breathe. They are completely unaware of which direction to go. It is completely overwhelming.

However, it is only through faith and action that you can survive a sandstorm. Your faith tells you that the sandstorm will end and that you can survive if you choose to.

Action prompts you to do the critical things necessary to ensure your ability to survive.

Likewise, you must have faith and you must take action in your life, even when you think you cannot. You must believe that you can become who or what you are called to, through faith and action, backed by a plan.

When you encounter the worst of life's events or circumstances and you feel overwhelmed and lost, that is when you are called to find your strength in the Lord. You must rely on your faith and confess that He is with you. Acknowledge that He is taking you and leading you through whatever it is that you are experiencing.

Once you can trust in that Faith, or even start to believe, then you must take action. God's plan for our life can only be activated when we take action to follow the path that He has laid out for us.

The Bible tells us that: Jesus looked at them and said, **"With man this is impossible, but with God all things are possible." Matthew 19:26**

We cannot possibly comprehend how God can provide for us and make things possible when we look from the perspective of a person. When your faith is lacking and you cannot see how any solution for you is possible; consider these truths:

- God is not a man, He is God. He can do whatever He needs to, according to His purpose and His will.
- All limitations in this world are very apparent and measurable. With God, there are no limitations.
- We have a beginning and an end. God is limitless and timeless.

If that isn't good enough for you, consider that man is not capable of consistently regulating the weather, seasons, the sun, moon and stars and....life. God can and does.

The required components to finding our own purpose reside in our faith in God and His will for our life. These are partnered with our desire and ability to take action.

"Worry and fear are like sandstorms.
They can be painful and can prevent you
from thinking of or
Even from seeing your goals.
But worry and fear, like sandstorms,
will soon pass."

Define Your Goals

Having faith and taking action only become relevant when you know where you are going. If you are starting to understand your purpose in life, through listening to what God is telling you, then you will start to develop your goals.

All goals usually start with a dream, but not all dreams will become goals. A goal is a written target to attain with a deadline.

If you feel that your purpose is to become a police officer, for example, then you might start with a goal of getting in shape. You might also have a goal of applying to a police academy by a certain date. Goals are the incentives that bring reality to our otherwise routine lives.

When I knew that my purpose was to be a motivational speaker, I set a goal to lose weight. There was an additional 40 pounds of Mike Rodriguez that I didn't want "hanging" around. I started my "getting in shape plan" on January 2. My initial plan was to lose 20 lbs. by June 28, which was approximately 3.5 pounds a month. That was realistic and manageable to me. I started my plan and lost 8 lbs. my first month alone! I was ahead of schedule, fired up and feeling good!

When June 28 rolled around, I had lost a total of 25 lbs.! (At the end of that same year I lost a total of 45 lbs.!) I felt great about losing my weight, but I felt so much better about exceeding my goal.

When you set your own goals, make sure that you follow a similar formula:

- Have a specific goal
- Make sure your goal is realistic
- Make sure your goal is manageable
- Make sure your goal is written
- Your goal must have an end date or it will stay a dream.

Eliminate these non-committal words: I'd like to, I hope to, I want to, I plan on and "one day," etc.
Instead say I WILL and I COMMIT!
Saying binding words is liberating and causes your mind to start "owning" your goal. It will become real, because it is real to you.
It will be your own, so…..OWN IT!

"Goals are the incentives that bring reality to our otherwise routine lives."

What About Failure?

Ask anyone you know if they have dreams for their life. Of Course the majority will admit that they do. Now ask if they are pursuing those dreams with a goal and most will say that they aren't, followed by a heartfelt explanation of why they aren't. Anything worth pursing will always come with three things:

1. Hard work during the process,
2. Great satisfaction when it is accomplished, and
3. Failure along the way.

The truth is that most of us don't pursue our most passionate goals because of either the risk of failure or a previous encounter with failure that killed the dream completely.

Expect failure. Just look at it differently. Plan on it and get ready to face it and work through it. Anything worthwhile will take time, great efforts and will require adjusting along the way. This means that you will encounter challenges along the way. Failure is a necessary and important part of the developmental process in any endeavor. This is how we learn to improve and how we learn to grow.

If you have started a healthy eating plan, you might slip up and gain a pound or 2. That is ok; it is not ok to quit.

When you start any endeavor, the challenge of facing something new will bring excitement and uncertainty. This is normal and is a part of growing. However, when your emotions turn to defeat, you must remember and reach back into that excitement, to keep your hope active!

Consider this, if you choose to never get started because of potential failure, then you will always be where you are. The question is can you live with that?

Also, if you choose to get started and you encounter a failure, these are the situations that God gives us to prepare us for even greater challenges in our future. This is why you feel the excitement to begin with! He is speaking to you.

Failure defines an event, not a person. This is true to every situation in your life. You may have done things wrong or you may not be at a place in your life where you want to be, but YOU ARE NOT A FAILURE!

To the contrary, YOU are full of untapped potential, just waiting to be used! Recognize that failure is only a temporary situation to learn from in any endeavor. To keep going will require mental strength, focus and a positive attitude!

When you fail, it will be easy to make excuses and it will be easier to start believing them! Be honest and true to both yourself and to your goals!

The final ingredients will be to overcome your emotions and to overcome your excuses. Do this by tapping into your true faith. Set goals and take immediate action after you encounter any failure.

Do not let excuses define your limits!

POSITIVE AFFIRMATIONS:
- ➢ I will Say "I Can," and "I Will"
- ➢ I will claim victory.
- ➢ I will no longer try, I will commit and find a way.
- ➢ I will start believing and saying that through faith and action, all things are possible, as long as it is God's will.
- ➢ I will write my goals down.
- ➢ I understand that failure is an event, I am not a failure.
- ➢ I will learn from my mistakes.
- ➢ I will keep going and I WILL become better.
- ➢ Excuses will not define my limits!

Chapter 6

Finding Clarity

"But seek first His kingdom
and His righteousness,
and all these things will be given to you"
-    Matthew 6:33

CHAPTER 6 – Finding CLARITY

Working to improve your life is not an easy task.

It is, after all, your life that we are talking about. Just as you would never start to drive a car with dirty, foggy or unclear windows, you should never live your life with a dirty, foggy or an unclear mindset. Your mind needs clarity.

1. You need to think, understand and reason to make the right decisions.
2. You will also need people in your life that share these same principles and values. People who will provide you with counsel, wisdom and guidance.
3. You need to remove the bad habits, people and things in your life that are holding you back. I call this baggage.

When I made the decision to identify and remove my baggage, it was a double bonus. Amazingly, I started to get closer to God and my life started to get better! When you remove the things in your life that hold you to a limited mindset or to your problems, the clarity that comes with it is unbelievable.

I often compare my ability to see things now, with how things look through 3D glasses. Without 3D glasses, the movie is blurry. You can make it out and you can even watch it, but the journey is not as pleasant as it was even meant to be. You might even give yourself a headache!

When I removed my baggage and became closer in my faith, it was like putting on 3D glasses for my life. I started seeing things clearer. I could identify problems in my life, the right solutions and the right people. Most importantly, the journey has become pleasant, as it was meant to be.

Giving Up Baggage

As you continue your own journey through life, you will become more aware of your strengths and who you are. You also start to recognize the things that are holding you back or that may not be aligning you with your purpose. This is going to be very different for everyone. Each one of us has our own struggles, our own personal issues and things that hold us back.

All of these things can and will prevent us from sharing our gifts. Most issues start innocently enough, but as we continue to keep them in our lives, they continue to grow. Then we might start believing that they are a part of us. You must know and believe that they are not.

Our God is righteous, pure and holy. Nothing that He creates comes with baggage. I call it baggage, because we are the ones that pick up the bad habits and carry them around.

We say and do the wrong things and think unhealthy thoughts. Then we carry this "baggage" around with us, sometimes throughout our entire lives. This is not natural and isn't the way it is meant to be. If you are experiencing a negative situation in your life, due to whatever baggage that you are carrying, I plead with you today to find the strength to do this: Let it go and give it up. Any baggage that you are carrying is heavy. It is a burden and will slow you down.

You must completely give up whatever you have in your life that is keeping you from stepping into your potential. You might say, well there is nothing meant for me anyway. That is only your baggage talking to you. It doesn't want you to let it go. It will work to deceive you and maybe even convince you that you are the way you are. It's not true.

Don't be afraid of what you can be; be more afraid of what "won't" be, then turn that fear into strength! When you are in a bad spot, you must remember that you didn't get there easily, so you might not get out easily. Everything takes time and so will moving yourself to a better place. Learn patience and understand that as long as you keep doing the right things every day, your life will get better!

Don't be afraid, don't worry and don't consider any negative "what ifs." Only think positive "what ifs" and tell yourself, "What if I succeed?" Remind yourself how you will improve and how your life will improve!

Our God is not an author of fear, worry, deception or uncertainty. Consider this, worrying is actually your own mind hyper thinking about potential outcomes. It consistently dwells on these fictitious outcomes that usually never happen.

Once you give up something, you need to take action to replace it with something else that will have a positive impact on your life. If you don't, you might be tempted to go back and start picking up your old baggage again. For example, if you stop smoking, you might choose to replace it by starting to work out. This positive replacement will keep you focused and healthy, pushing you to stay on the right track.

God is pure, holy and righteous. Let him work in your life to remove the things that are not in line with His will of your life. View everything that is in your life as either:

1. A stepping stone that is helping to bring you closer to God and to your purpose, or
2. Heavy Baggage that is slowing you down or keeping you from even getting to your destination.

He has a plan for you and you must find the strength to give up whatever it is that is holding you back from realizing your greatness!

Mid-Life ~~Crisis~~ Purpose

If you are not realizing your purpose, you will know it. You will feel like something is missing from your life and you will be right. This is how the Holy Spirit works through us.

Earlier we talked about how God has already shown you who you are. You were created with your talents, skills and desires from the day that you were born. Consider that if there is a God and if He is the creator of everything, then of course He would have designed you with purpose, desires and abilities.

This would conclude that since every exterior feature on our body has purpose and functionality for us to exist and survive, so does your internal mind and spirit.

I'm convinced that as we live our life and as we go through the experiences of this world, that God is always with us and He is pushing us to our true purpose. If we don't listen, and if we aren't obedient, we will get lost. Although our physical body and mind might be separated from Christ, our soul is always in contact. Because of this, I believe that mid-life crisis is not how we should define what happens to us in mid-life. My experience has shown me that when most people hit their mid-life, that is when they are most likely to have matured and are the most willing to listen to God and to their heart's true desires.

You can start feeling what you have known and felt inside of you all of your life. Now, you just might be more willing, more able and more importantly, more prepared to pursue your true purpose.

To me, this is why you see and hear so many people adjust careers or do something that is perceived as "radical" in their mid-life. I don't believe that it is because they are unstable or that they are looking to reconnect with their youth, I believe that they are finally able to act on the internal desire that has been in their heart and mind since the day they were born. They are being called to their true purpose. Your current or previous career is important, because it was preparing you for where you need to go. I have come to this conclusion, because of what I have lived through in my own life, and from what I have seen in others.

You might know someone who is in a job or industry for many years and you might think that they are very happy. Then, one day out of the blue, they might tell you that they have quit their job to move to another industry or to even start their own business.

The natural response, is to say they are going through mid-life crisis. As a result, others might want to talk them out of it, primarily because it is different, and it makes other people feel uncomfortable.

Instead, I would say that they might be going through "Mid-Life Purpose!"

It might be considered a crisis for the sole purpose that it shakes up the standard of what everyone else thinks, but that is the beauty in this. God created each one of us with our own calling, so we are all different in that sense.

When you trust God and you know what you feel, then at the same time you must trust that He is responsibly guiding you and that He has a plan for you.

> ## *"He must become greater. I must become less."*
> ### *John 3:30*

If you go through Mid-Life "Purpose," consider that you might just be feeling what you have known all of your life. That internal feeling may be calling you to adjust your predefined life's path to your purpose.

This doesn't mean that your life has been a waste. To the contrary, it provided you with people, opportunities, resources, skill refinement and so much more.

To ensure that this is relevant to you, make sure that you are praying, that your intentions are good, and that your path is aligned properly with your true passion. Make sure that your end results will responsibly benefit others, not just you.

Planting Seeds

You are planting seeds throughout your life in everything that you do, say and think. If you are planting good seeds, based on positive influence, these seeds will start to grow in a positive way. Likewise, if you are planting bad seeds, through negative influence, they will grow in a similar manner. Each encounter with someone today, is a seed planted that may grow into something good or bad tomorrow. Sometimes, it might not grow into anything at all. When you focus on serving others, you naturally start planting good seeds.

I can recall numerous times in my life where I had unknowingly planted positive seeds with someone through a conversation or an interaction. When you do something right, it always feels right. That is your conviction telling you "yes, this is what I should be doing."

Years ago my sweet wife Bonnie took over the Box Tops program at my daughter's elementary school. Bonnie is a great administrator, but doesn't like to speak in front of groups. She asked me to volunteer my time for the program, to be the announcer at the school assembly each Friday.

She said that the program would require about an hour or so of my time each week. I love my wife and would do anything for her, but I must admit that initially I didn't want to do it. I thought attending the program each week would be an inconvenience for me, so I concluded that it wouldn't be a productive use of my time. During that point in my life I was in corporate America, and I felt that it was very important to keep business as a priority.
I was going to say no.

I didn't feel good about my decision, because both of my oldest daughters had a great experience at the school and they loved it. The staff and the education at Sparks Elementary are second to none.

After talking with my wonderful wife, she helped me to look at the situation differently. She asked me to not think that I was creating more work, but to look at it as though I was giving back to the school. That made sense and caused a good "spark" to ignite in me. As a result, I changed my mind and agreed to help out.

Every Friday morning, I would show up at the school assembly with my daughter Linsey as my helper. We would encourage the kids, announce winners and give awards. I ended up volunteering for the entire year. It was the first investment of my time that I had ever given without financial gain, and I absolutely loved it. I looked forward to going every Friday and I was known throughout the School as "The Box Tops Guy."

When I had to give up the role, I was really sad.
The final day, all of the kids made a giant card and everyone signed it. It was awesome. Ironically, just a year earlier I was viewing this as a potential burden, and now here I was feeling sad about letting it go.

I had learned a valuable lesson that Zig Ziglar had shared for years: "You can have everything in life you want, if you will just help enough other people get what they want."

In my situation, I had helped my wife, the school and the students to get what they wanted, someone to host the Box Tops Program; and they, unknowingly, gave me the gift to realize unselfishness and the importance of giving back.

This would be another gift that was always in me, that I just needed to start using. God was still preparing me for my Purpose. In addition, I was also planting seeds with the people that I came in contact with, including my own wife!

I have great relationships with the staff at that school to this day. I see them often now that my daughter Leia attends Sparks. London, my youngest, will be attending as well.

In addition, there were many times that I would be out in Frisco, my home city, and a young boy or girl would approach me with a gigantic smile and say, "Hey I know you, YOU are the Box Tops guy!" What a great feeling. The memories and those feelings of helping are priceless.

When you meet others in your life, you might come in contact with them later on as well. How will they remember you? What will that interaction create for the future? Are you planting the right seeds that will grow and become productive? God may put someone in your life today, to plant a seed with you for the future.

I cannot tell you how many times I have interacted with people to only be in a situation later in life where they needed something from me or I needed something from them. It sure is great when that happens, to know that you made good choices years prior.

Also remember, that if you don't take care of your seeds, they won't grow. This means to invest time, share smiles and learn to give to others, by having a peaceful and giving mindset with full clarity.

POSITIVE AFFIRMATIONS:

- ➤ I will think, speak and act, in a right way.
- ➤ I will identify and remove the baggage in my life that I am carrying around.
- ➤ I will give up bad habits that keep me from my true potential.
- ➤ I will acknowledge and embrace my talents.
- ➤ I will learn to recognize opportunities that are presented and I will seize them.
- ➤ Fear will not dictate my life, as our father is not an author of fear.
- ➤ I will have a giving heart and mindset.
- ➤ I will keep my thoughts pure, so I will think clearly.

Chapter 7

Standing Strong

"Let not the opinions of man interfere with the directions given to you by God."
- Unknown

CHAPTER 7 – Standing STRONG

Earlier we learned that through faith and action, all things are possible. But how do we develop our faith?

One way to develop your faith is to start by trusting in God. Trust that your life is in His care and under His control. Trust that you have already been given all that you need to prevail to find your WHY.

What Are your Strengths?

You were designed, not by chance but by choice. Your birth was a miracle and your creation is a testament that you are called to this world to serve a higher purpose. God does not make mistakes, nor are you ever left to fend for yourself in this life all alone.

As we enter this world and develop, the natural tendency is to only make note of the visible element of who we are. We focus on the physical: our eyes, hands, heart, lungs, brain, etc., but there is much more to who we are. All of these physical traits were designed and given to use for very precise reasons. Your eyes to see, your fingers to grasp, legs to walk, a system to eliminate waste and even another to reproduce. These physical gifts did not happen by chance.

Recognize that we are also given spiritual gifts. As we mature, we can start to see these gifts reveal themselves through our interests, talents and desires. These are signs that can lead us to our purpose. They can also give us the strength to draw on when we go through tough times. How we think, how we learn, what we desire, skills we recognize and talents that we share, are all examples.

As you start or continue to pursue your purpose, be aware of who you are and what you are being called to do. This means knowing your personality traits, your strengths, your weaknesses and your potential to pursue things that might make you fail. Your internal drive and desire to do something is the start of listening for your purpose. Ask yourself "What are the strengths that I possess that are relevant to this purpose I am feeling?

In addition to physical and spiritual gifts, God also introduces us to "other people" as gifts, to help us along our way. I consider my wife Bonnie and my daughters to all be gifts from God. They are another purpose in my life that has continued to push me. My family is in my heart and in my mind daily. They are my strength and motivation to work when I want to give up. They are the love that I feel when I am sad and they are the encouragers in my life all of the time.

Know your strengths, because they can also lead you and push you directly to your purpose, or they very well may actually BE your purpose!

When you focus on your strengths, you start to build a core confidence that you will need throughout your life. This is very important because your ability to prevail during any weakness, will be determined by the strength that you have already developed. Your ability to be successful is dependent on your perseverance through your faith, and it is also dependent on your ability to continue to find strength by taking action.

Go through challenges head on. If you are in a challenge now, know that it is only temporary. With proper planning, true faith and by taking action, you will find the strength to keep going.

Making Gods Priorities Yours (Parable of the Talents)

At this point you should have a very firm understanding that God does indeed have a plan for your life, and He has equipped you with the strengths necessary to fulfill your purpose. You should also know that it is your responsibility to understand and take action to pursue that plan, to discover your purpose.

God's priorities are for you to live your life for His glory, while managing your free will. You might struggle between following His priorities and following YOUR priorities.

When we follow our own agendas and priorities, based on what we think and feel, we might be acting against God's priorities. So how do we know if we are following God's priorities? A start is to follow His word and His Truth. This simply means doing what God expects us to do: The Right Things. Sometimes, however, what seems right to us is clearly the wrong thing.

Here is a version of The Parable of the Talents from the Bible, to clarify further:

"For it will be like a man going on a journey, who called his servants and entrusted to them his property. To one he gave five talents, to another two, to another one, to each according to his ability. Then he left for his journey.

The servant who had received the five talents went at once and traded with them, and he made five talents more. The servant who received two talents also increased his and made two talents more. However, the servant who had received the one talent went and dug in the ground and hid his master's money.

Now after a long time the master of those servants came home and asked to settle the accounts with each servant. He who had received the five talents came forward, bringing five talents more, saying: 'Master, you gave to me five talents; here I have made five talents more.' His master said to him, 'Well done, good and faithful servant. You have been faithful over a little; I will set you over much. Enter into the joy of your master.'

Then the one who had the two talents came forward, saying, 'Master, you delivered to me two talents; here I have made two talents more.' His master said to him, 'Well done, good and faithful servant. You have been faithful over a little; I will set you over much. Enter into the joy of your master.'

Then, the servant who had received the one talent came forward, saying, 'Master, I knew you to be a hard man, reaping where you did not sow, and gathering where you scattered no seed, so I was afraid, and I went and hid your talent in the ground. Here you have exactly what is yours: one talent.' But his master answered him, 'you wicked and slothful servant! You knew that I reap where I have not sown and gather where I scattered no seed?

Then you ought to have invested my money with the bankers, and at my coming I should have received what was my own with interest.

The Master then took the single talent from the servant and gave it to the servant who had created the ten talents.

"For to everyone who has, will more be given, and he will have an abundance. But from the one who has not, even what he has will be taken away. And cast the worthless servant into the outer darkness."

In the Parable of the Talents, the word "talent" is used to describe a form of currency. However, after reading this, it is easy to see that you can change the definition of Talent, to mean that of a skill or aptitude, and you can still use this same lesson as outlined in the story. God's priorities are for you to live your life according to his will and to prosper. He will provide you with the "talents" (the means and the way), but you must still take action and properly use those "talents" (skills) that He has equipped you with.

When you are aware of a skill you possess and put your actions on hold, you are in effect, burying those talents. You might say, I want to do this, but what if I fail?

Or "I can't do that in my life right now." You might even say things like I said, "Who am I to do this? I'm afraid of what might happen, so I'll just be cautious!"

This is where faith comes in. You must make responsible, faith-based decisions to ensure that your priorities are in line with God's priorities, then you must take action. Overcome your fears and doubts and use what he has given you! Make sure you are aligned in your life with people who lift you up in all areas of your life.

Who is influencing you?

"A smile and a few nice words can be given by anyone. It takes true character and integrity to back your words with action."

This is a very easy subject to understand when you are following the right path, with the right people, because God's word gives us clarity.
When we follow the truth, it is easy to do the right things.

The irony is that it is very difficult to see when you are being influenced negatively by people that you like and trust.

Being educated by someone on life situations to know right from wrong, and personally experiencing situations in your life, can be two very different things.

Here is why.
When you are taught life lessons, you are learning from a third party perspective. Although you might conceptually and morally understand the lesson, it still isn't your own experience. I say this because since you have not and are not actually living the situation, you don't have any emotional ties, an actual experience or investment in the situation.

We should use logic and truth to assess any situation. This can be a positive thing that will give us the ability to see any situation objectively, IF and only IF we remember the facts, or the "truths" about the situation.

Now here is the challenge with experiencing life's situations. They don't just happen suddenly and they don't just happen with strangers. They develop over time, with people that we learn to like and trust. When you are involved with people and situations, the variables change, because you become emotionally attached to the people and the situation. You are now dealing with real people that you might be friends with and even care deeply about. The stakes will change, because your emotions will over-rule your logic.

116

From this perspective, you can understand why people make poor choices about other people and situations that can have a negative influence on their life.

This is how we can have friends and family, people that we care about, who talk us out of our dreams or talk us into bad situations!

A friend of mine was recently telling me about his college son. He was raised in a loving, Christian home where they frequently talked about life, life's challenges and making the right choices. He mentioned that they all had a strong core set of values and morals. In fact, he often talked with his son about his career and goals, and the risks of drugs, alcohol and sex. His son knew the risks of these matters and assured his father that he would never be influenced to do those types of things. However, shortly after starting school, he met a girl that he started developing feelings for. His emotions took over and his logic was pushed to the back seat.

Now, because he liked and trusted this girl, he was doing things that he knew he shouldn't be doing. His grades were being affected, which would ultimately impact his career. However, because he liked the girl and he thought that she was a "good person," he felt that it all was ok, even though in his heart he knew what he was doing was wrong.
He was being short sighted.

The smart, Christian boy who once assured his father that he would use common sense and truth of his faith to follow the right path, was now following the wrong path.

In addition, he was justifying it, because of his emotions for someone else.

This is a prime example of how you can be influenced by people. A smile and a few nice words can be given by anyone. They might even be super nice, really cute and even funny, and not seem like the wrong kind of people! It takes true character and integrity to back words and smiles with the truth of character of action. Don't just listen to the words people use, pay attention to why they are saying them, and IF they are backing them in their walk. Anyone can say they are a Christian and they might be, but morals and values can and will have very different meanings to each person.

If you have someone in your life that you like and trust, yet they are asking you or influencing you to do things that aren't in your best interest, or aligned with your values and life goals, then you need to take a break and reevaluate that relationship. This is easier said than done, as it is difficult when you like someone and trust someone. Coincidentally, you might even enjoy the things you are doing and even know they are wrong. This still doesn't make it right.

This is where you step back, pray and follow the truth. Ask yourself if being in this relationship or friendship is getting you closer to or further from being the right person that you should be. Ask yourself if you can afford the risks of the consequences that the temporary feelings may bring to you, for the rest of your permanent life.

Being a mature person and being sound in your faith, doesn't mean that you are perfect, but it means that you can learn to discern temporary gratification from long term treasures.

This means learning to make the VERY tough decisions to either:

- Say no to the temporary situations and things that you may like, but you know are not good for you, or
- Run from the people and things that are tempting and influencing you if you can't say no.

Surround yourself with good people who do the right things. Your friends who do the wrong things won't like it, because darkness does not like the light. You might say "Mike, my friends are not dark or evil, they are good people!" My answer would be, "Truly Good people DO and cause others to "DO" Good things and to become better." This goes back to my earlier statement about letting our emotions override our logic and the truth.

119

There are very nice, funny and attractive people who do terrible things. Be kind to them and even pray with them, but certainly don't let them influence your life. You should be the one who is influencing them.

You will eventually become like the people you choose to hang around with, so why not hang out with people who have a positive influence on you; those who encourage you to do the right things and the best things for your life. Lift those up around you and be around those who lift you up.

You might only start with one person today, but pray and trust that God will bring the right people into your life.

You cannot afford to take unnecessary risks that can take you further away from your life's purpose.

You cannot afford any relationship that is compromising your health, wealth, well-being and other relationships.

True love is unselfish and encourages, guides and supports you to be the right person, do the right things and have the right value system. It is about respect, values, morals and conviction. Take time to seek counsel from those you trust, who are a positive example to others. Seek those who are grounded in their faith and who have life experiences and guidance to share with you.

"Learn to discern temporary gratification from long term treasures."

Finding Your Why

I started this book by saying, your life was given to you as a gift. Realizing this, each and every day, you should give thanks for your life. Every morning, the first person that you come in contact with is YOU, so make it a positive first encounter.

When you open your eyes the first thing in the morning, do this:

- Pray
- Smile
- Give thanks for all that you have, and
- Give thanks that you are alive.

Make a decision to be positive and to impact others positively. Recognize that because you are alive, that you still have work to do! Your journey has been and will continue to be unique to you; from the people you meet and the places you will go, to the experiences that you will have. Regardless of where you are in life's journey, seeing your life as a gift is a great starting point.

121

When you start to understand that your life's direction is influenced by your own decisions, you can feel empowered! The reality is that your life's purpose has already been defined. From the time you were born, you have been given a miracle. The miracle of life. God has already equipped you with all of the tools that you will need to succeed. You were given every emotion and skill to handle what life brings. You have what it takes and you are strong enough to make it through any and all circumstances. In addition, He has already tested all circumstances for you.

His promise is that He will never leave you nor forsake you. Know that He is always with you.

In my own life, through all of my twists and turns, I can clearly look back now and know that every situation had its purpose; to push me up or to push me through. Every encounter, every job, every challenge and blessing was meant to guide or correct my path to push me.

I may have wanted things to happen faster than they did, but they have always happened the way they were supposed to. Because of this, I am also able to understand that even though God's time frame is not the same as ours, we are always aligned with His. If you lose patience or if you get frustrated with delays, remember this: Tomorrow will come, next week is coming, next year, two years, five and ten years will indeed come.

Will you face the arrival of the future with regret or will you have the peace and confidence of knowing that you have stayed the course and did your part?

I have shared many thoughts, ideas and tools on "Finding your WHY." You have been given many gifts to succeed in this life. Every emotion you have and everything that He does, is good and is predetermined. We are the ones who complicate life by abusing the gifts that He has given us:

- Don't overuse fear, sadness and anger.
- Display your joy, happiness and love.
- Recognize your skills, talents and desires.
- Don't believe the doubt, fears and "what ifs."
- Listen to what He is telling you.
- Ask yourself "Why NOT ME?"
- Know what He has shown you.
- Don't listen to others in a worse place than you.
- Have Faith during good times and bad times.
- Give more than you take.

Your purpose has been predefined and your life is the vessel to fulfill it, so have faith and be strong! Take action today and every day and never give up! Learn to trust in His guidance through your overwhelming desire to follow a pure thought, dream or an idea that serves a purpose. This is how God communicates to us.

123

As you go through your wonderful and amazing gift of your life's journey, He indeed will always be with you. When you start with Christ as the foundation of your life, and you keep Him at the center of your life, you will find peace, true happiness and the WHY behind your purpose.

You might already feel, understand or even know your WHY, or to the contrary, you might even think to yourself: Who am I to do this?
What credentials or gifts do I have?

Don't burden yourself with negative thoughts. Instead, think limitless, take action, believe and let only God, not man, define your limits. Be willing to do whatever it takes to make your purpose a reality.

So, who are you?
You were given the gift of life by the one true King, THAT is who you are.

Now, it's time to find your WHY, so
"Go Forth and Make Your Life Exceptional!"

The ~~End~~ .....
New Beginning

"If it is God's will for you,

You will ultimately succeed."

-   Mike Rodriguez

Finding Your WHY

EPILOGUE

Throughout my life, I have always felt my WHY, but I have not always been in pursuit of it. Mostly because I have been my own biggest obstacle. I was often distracted by people and things in this world that kept me from stepping into my full potential. I knew there was a "bigger picture," I was just not focused enough to see it.

I was overweight for many years. I ate unhealthy and I drank alcohol irresponsibly. I did not follow my faith as I was supposed to. As a result, I dealt with the repercussions of being unhealthy spiritually, physically and mentally. I knew that drinking was the biggest obstacle that was keeping me from my relationship with God and from fulfilling my purpose. I needed to and wanted to remove it, so I completely turned it over to God. I still look back in complete and humbled amazement how He did that for me.

After years of very strong feelings that God had something better for me, I only took action to improve my life, when I chose to be aware of and act on God's plan. Through his grace I am a new man.

I understand my purpose and I am full of life. I can see Him clearly, and I am stronger than ever.

I have learned, through his word, that I must be healthy in three categories: spiritually, mentally and physically. These core life components will always be works in progress for me, however I am committed to my success.

With regards to success, I have always felt that my purpose was to help others through the gift of words. I have always dreamed of becoming a motivational/inspirational speaker, but for the largest part of my life, I only considered this a dream.
Who was I to be a speaker?
What credentials or gifts did I have?
These were negative thoughts that I burdened myself with.

So, who am I?
I am a son of our King.
I know Him and He knows me.

Today, all because of Him, and through my obedience, I am living my life's dream, my life's goal and most importantly, my life's purpose.....my WHY.

Believe in God and his plan for your life. Have faith and take action. You too will find your WHY.

About The Author

Mike Rodriguez is an internationally known professional speaker and trainer with the world famous Zig Ziglar Corporation. He is also a sales expert and a master sales trainer. Mike delivers performance-based seminars, following the principles learned in his own life and those learned from the philosophies of Zig Ziglar.

Everyone faces challenges; Mike believes that through faith and action, you can overcome the challenges in your life to attain your goals and become who you truly want to be.

Mike is a high-energy leader who has worked in corporate America since 1991 training, building, mentoring and developing top performing people within teams and businesses. Mike started as a struggling sales representative, with no experience or formal training. He worked his way up to become a top-performer and an award-winning sales leader. He has held a variety of positions including Director of Sales, Vice President of Sales and President/Founder of his own company Telnet, a business partner with Southwestern Bell (now AT&T).

Mike has won Chairman's Club Awards, Achiever's Club Awards, Manager of the Year and numerous vacation trips. He credits his faith, having a plan, taking action and never giving up for enabling him to prevail over many failures and adversities in his own life. Most importantly, he has always believed in his God-given potential.

Throughout his career, Mike has built productivity-driven training programs and managed multi-million dollar quotas. He has experience delivering powerful messages and creating personal development strategies for new and tenured companies and teams across many industries.

With over two decades of personal development and leadership experience in business and corporate sales, Mike has professionally trained and motivated hundreds of people on sales process management and life strategies. Mike Rodriguez dedicates his time helping people of all backgrounds to step into their potential through proven key principles that are life-impacting. He has a solid leadership approach and a passionate motivational attitude, backed by powerful and effective speaking.

Mike has been happily married since 1991 to the love of his life and together they have five beautiful daughters.

If you have the right attitude, you can have the right kind of success, regardless of the type of industry that you are in.

As an internationally known Speaker,
Mike has experience working with people
in all walks of life.
You can schedule Mike Rodriguez
to speak at your next event:

Go to:

www.MikeRodriguezResults.com

www.Ziglar.com

Also available by Mike Rodriguez:

8 Keys to Exceptional Selling
www.8KeystoExceptionalSelling.com

M.A.P. Selling
www.MAPselling.com

Selling is Like Dating
www.SellingisLikeDating.com

.

MIKE'S PAGE OF GRATITUDE
Those who have had a major impact on my life:

Bonnie Rodriguez
Helen Rodriguez
Antonio Rodriguez
Bill Malmer
Sharon Malmer
Lauren Rodriguez
Lexi Rodriguez
Linsey Rodriguez
Leia Rodriguez
London Rodriguez
Steven Rodriguez
Tony Rodriguez
Sheri Gwatney
Diane Bevan
Todd Pennington
Zig Ziglar
Tom Ziglar
Og Mandino
Brian Tracy
Jim Rohn
John Maxwell
Jeff Tousa
Angeles Ramos
Greg Benedek
John Czapko

Disclaimer & Copyright Information

Mike and Bonnie 1991

Mike and Bonnie 2014

I can do **ALL THINGS** through Christ

who strengthens me.

Philippians 4:13

………..now go and find your WHY!

9 780990 600121